MOTHER

"Family faces are magic mirrors. Looking at people who belong to us we see the past, present & future." ♥ Gail Lumet Buckley

For

From

♥

And so it begins...

Your date and place of birth:

_____

_____

Your parents' names, birthdates, and places of birth:

_____

_____

_____

_____

_____

_____

Your brothers and sisters, from oldest to youngest:

_____

_____

_____

_____

_____

_____

_____

How did your parents choose your name?

_____

_____

_____

_____

_____

_____

_____

Childhood...

Which memories from your youngest years stand out?

_____

_____

_____

_____

_____

_____

_____

_____

_____

_____

_____

_____

_____

_____

_____

_____

_____

_____

_____

_____

_____

_____

_____

What kind of child were you?

_____
_____

WHAT ONE LOVES IN CHILDHOOD STAYS IN THE HEART FOREVER.

_____
_____
_____
_____
_____
_____
_____

_____
_____
_____
_____
_____
_____
_____
_____
_____
_____
_____

Me!

What do you remember about your mom and dad?

_____

_____

_____

_____

_____

_____

_____

_____

_____

_____

_____

_____

Mom & dad

What did your mom and dad do for a living?

Where did your family go on VACATION?

What were your favorite foods?

All the things I really like to do are immoral, illegal, or fattening. ♡

What was the family car? What do you remember most about it?

_____

_____

_____

_____

_____

Were there any magical places in your childhood home you remember?

_____

_____

_____

_____

_____

_____

_____

_____

_____

_____

_____

What was your room like?

_____

_____

_____

_____

_____

_____

_____

_____

Did you keep your room clean? (Of course you did!)

_____

_____

_____

_____

_____

_____

_____

_____

_____

_____

_____

_____

Did you have pets? Tell me about them.

A SOFT FURRY WARM TOASTY
FRIENDLY LITTLE PETTY-PET
OF YOUR OWN IS A MUST ♥.

Your Family Pet

Did you help out around the house? Did you get an allowance?

_____

_____

_____

_____

_____

_____

Did you have other ways of earning money?

_____

_____

_____

HOUSEWORK,
when done
correctly,
can kill you.

_____

_____

_____

_____

_____

_____

_____

_____

_____

_____

_____

_____

_____

What were your favorite pastimes?

_____

_____

_____

_____

_____

_____

_____

_____

_____

_____

_____

_____

_____

_____

_____

_____

_____

_____

_____

_____

_____

What was your favorite childhood book?

_____

_____

_____

_____

_____

_____

_____

_____

_____

_____

What were your favorite TV shows?

_____

_____

_____

_____

_____

_____

_____

_____

_____

_____

_____

_____

_____

_____

Describe your favorite outfit.

_____
_____
_____
_____
_____
_____
_____
_____
_____
_____
_____
_____
_____

What were your favorite accessories?

_____
_____
_____
_____
_____
_____
_____
_____

I BELIEVE IN ACCESSORIES.

What were your favorite games?

_____
_____
_____
_____
_____
_____
_____
_____
_____

Describe a favorite toy.

_____
_____
_____
_____
_____
_____
_____
_____
_____
_____

Who were your childhood friends?

_____

_____

_____

_____

_____

_____

_____

_____

_____

_____

_____

_____

_____

_____

_____

Where did they live?

_____

_____

_____

_____

_____

_____

When did you first spend the night at a friend's house? Were you scared?

_____

_____

_____

_____

_____

Tell me a sleepover story from that time.

_____

_____

_____

_____

_____

_____

_____

_____

_____

_____

_____

"FRIENDS ~
They are kind to each other's HOPES.
They cherish each other's DREAMS."
Thoreau

What was your first school?

_____

_____

_____

_____

_____

_____

_____

_____

Who was your favorite elementary school teacher, and why?

_____

_____

_____

_____

_____

_____

_____

_____

_____

School days

Describe a typical school day.

_____

_____

_____

_____

_____

_____

_____

_____

Picture Perfect

Did you participate in any special school events?

What did you do during the summer?

Did you play make-believe? What did you like to pretend?

_____

_____

_____

_____

_____

_____

_____

_____

_____

_____

_____

_____

_____

_____

_____

_____

_____

_____

_____

_____

_____

_____

_____

Describe a typical Saturday.

Tell me a FAMILY story or two...

Remember...

_____

_____

_____

_____

_____

_____

_____

_____

♥ Special Times ♥

Growing up...

What did you dream about while growing up?

_____

_____

_____

_____

_____

_____

_____

_____

_____

_____

_____

_____

_____

_____

_____

_____

_____

_____

_____

Memories. . . the food of our childhood, food that meant love. ♥

Did you like school?

_____

_____

_____

_____

How did you get to school?

_____

_____

_____

_____

SchOoL
Picture

How did you get ready for school? What did you wear?

_____

_____

_____

_____

_____

_____

_____

_____

_____

Me! ♥

Did you use makeup? Nail polish?

_____

_____

_____

_____

_____

_____

How did you do your hair?

_____

_____

_____

_____

_____

_____

_____

_____

_____

SMART,
PRETTY
& TALENTED...

What was your favorite subject, and why?

Which teacher inspired you the most?

_____

_____   CHARMING,
                                                    FUNNY &
_____   BRILLIANT. ♥
                                                      YES!
_____

_____

_____

_____

_____

_____

_____

Which teacher do you wish you had stood up to?

_____

_____

_____

_____

_____

_____

_____

_____

_____

_____

_____

_____

Did you belong to any school clubs?

Were you on any sports teams? Tell me about an important game.

TEAM
picture

Did you ever ditch school?

_____

_____

_____

_____

_____

_____

_____

What was the worst thing you got in trouble for in high school?

_____

_____

_____

_____

_____

_____

_____

_____

_____

_____

_____

_____

What was the biggest thing you remember happening in our country
when you were in high school?

_____

_____

_____

_____

_____

_____

_____

Did you pay attention to politics or what was going on in the world?

_____

_____

_____

_____

_____

_____

_____

_____

_____

_____

Did you keep a diary or journal then? Do you still have it?

Did you make money in high school? How?

THE BEST THINGS
IN LIFE
ARE FREE.

Who taught you how to drive? What was that like?

_____

_____

_____

_____

_____

_____

_____

Tell me about getting your driver's license.

_____

_____

_____

_____

_____

_____

_____

_____

_____

_____

_____

What was your first car?

_____

How much did a gallon of gas cost then? Did you do a lot of driving?

_____
_____
_____
_____
_____
_____
_____
_____
_____
_____
_____
_____

sing in THE CAR
_____
_____
_____
_____
_____

Did you go to dances and parties? What were they like?

_____

_____

_____

_____

_____

_____

_____

_____

_____

What did everyone wear?

_____

_____

_____

_____

_____

_____

_____

_____

_____ ❋ So much Fun! ❋ _____

How did everyone dance, or did they? What was the music like?

GOOD·FRIENDS

Who was your best friend?

_____

_____

How did you meet?

_____

_____

_____

_____

_____

_____

_____

_____

_____

Tell me about a best friend adventure.

_____

_____

_____

_____

_____

_____

_____

_____

_____

_____

_____

_____

_____

_____

_____

_____

_____

_____

_____

_____

_____

"'Stay' is a charming word
in a friend's vocabulary."
♥ Louisa May Alcott

What was your social life like?

_____

_____

_____

_____

_____

_____

_____

_____

Who did you hang out with the most?

_____

_____

_____

_____

_____

_____

_____

_____

_____

_____

_____

_____

Tell me about something that made you laugh until you cried.

_____

_____

_____

_____

_____

_____

_____

_____

_____

_____

_____

_____

_____

_____

_____

_____

_____

_____

"FUNNY STUFF"

You were sooooo funny!

Tell me about your first date. (Who was your date? Where did you go? How old were you? What did you do? Do you remember what you wore? Details please, Mom.)

Did you like fashion magazines? If not, what did you read for fun?

♡ ALL YOUR FAVORITES.

Who were your favorite movie stars? Movies?

How about music? What did you like? ♫♪♫ ♫♪ ♫♫

_____

_____

_____

_____

_____

_____

_____

What was your favorite song, and why?

_____

_____

_____

_____

_____

_____

_____

_____

_____

_____

_____

Did you go to concerts? Tell me about your favorite ones.

♫♪♫
OH HAPPY DAY!

What did you have then that we don't use anymore?

What was an exciting invention of the day?

As you matured, what kinds of things inspired you?

Tell me about your high school dreams.

_____

_____

_____

_____

_____

_____

_____

_____

_____

_____

_____

_____

_____

_____

_____

_____

_____

_____

_____

_____

_____

_____

Do you use anything you learned in high school in your grown-up life?

How are you the same now as you were when you were a teenager?

_____

_____

_____

_____

_____

_____

_____

_____

_____

_____

_____

_____

_____

_____

_____

_____

_____

_____

KEEPING A
POSITIVE
ATTITUDE

On your own...

Did you ever think about what kind of house you wanted some day?

Or where you might live?

BLESSINGS

_____

_____

_____

_____

_____

_____

_____

_____

_____

_____

_____

_____

_____

_____

_____

_____

_____

_____

_____

_____

How old were you when you moved out of the house? Where did you go?

What was your place like? Did you live alone?

How did you like being on your own?

_____

_____

_____

_____

_____

_____

_____

_____

What did you miss most from living at home?

_____

_____

_____

_____

_____

_____

_____

_____

_____

_____

_____

_____

_____

When did you first feel like a grown-up?

_____

_____

_____

_____

_____

_____

_____

_____

_____

_____

_____

_____

_____

_____

_____

_____

_____

_____

_____

_____

_____

What was your first job? How much did you make? What did you do?

_____

_____

_____

_____

_____

_____

_____

_____

_____

_____

_____

_____

_____

_____

_____

_____

_____

_____

_____

_____

_____

What was your worst job ever?

Which job did you like best, and why?

DO STUFF WITH GUSTO

What did you do for fun?

_____ _____
_____
_____
_____
_____
_____
_____
_____
_____
_____
_____
_____
_____
_____
_____
_____
_____
_____
_____ FUN FUN FUN _____

Did you take any big trips?

Share some stories from that time.

Perfect
Day

Write a page or two about the loves in your life. Start at the beginning, please.

The love in your heart
wasn't put there to stay,
love isn't love
till it's
given
away.

Did you ever experience love at first sight? Did it work out?

(c o o)

L O V E   B I R D S

Tell me about the most romantic date you ever went on.

MR. WONDERFUL

Write about the one that got away.

Hours fly
Flowers die
New days
New ways
Pass by
Love stays

Starting a family...

Write about my dad. Tell me how you met him.

Mom & dad

Tell me about your first home together.

LIFE IS GOOD

What is your best advice about relationships?

_____

_____

_____

_____

_____

_____

_____

_____

_____

_____

_____

_____

_____

_____

_____

_____

_____

_____

_____

_____

_____

_____ *"Love is friendship set to music."*
                                    Anonymous ♥

Did you work? How was that part of your life going?

_____

_____

_____

_____

_____

_____

_____

_____

_____

_____

_____

_____

_____

_____

_____

_____

_____

_____

_____

_____

_____

_____

_____

_____

Tell me about finding out you were going to have me.

_____

_____

_____

_____

_____

_____

_____

_____

_____

_____

_____

_____

_____

_____

_____

_____

_____

_____

_____

_____   (I'm pregnant!)

Who did you tell first?

How were those nine months?

_____

_____

_____

_____

_____

_____

_____

_____

_____

_____

_____

_____

_____

_____

_____

_____

_____

_____

_____

_____

_____

_____

Based on your pregnancy, did you have any ideas about what kind of person I would be?

_____

_____

_____

_____

_____

_____

_____

_____

_____

_____

_____

_____

_____

_____

_____

_____

_____

_____

_____

_____

_____

_____

Did you like to eat anything interesting while you were pregnant?

Pickles & _Ice Cream_

What was your favorite maternity outfit?

On the day I was born...

How did it feel the first time you held me?

Me!

How was I most challenging as a baby?

_____ _____
_____
_____
_____
_____
_____
_____
_____
_____
_____
_____
_____
_____
_____
_____
_____
_____
_____
                              _____
                              _____
                              _____

What is your favorite story from when I was a baby?

How did your own mom, my grandma, affect your motherhood?

How did your dad, my grandpa, affect you as a mom?

Do you feel like a good mother?

_____

_____

_____

_____

_____

_____

_____

_____

_____

_____

_____

_____

_____

_____

_____

_____

_____

_____

"IF YOU DON'T WANT YOUR CHILDREN TO HEAR WHAT YOU'RE SAYING, PRETEND YOU'RE TALKING TO THEM." ♥ ANON.

A picture is worth a thousand words.

How do I remind you of yourself when you were my age?

_____
_____
_____
_____
_____
_____
_____
_____
_____
_____
_____
_____

Do you miss having little children?

_____
_____
_____
_____
_____
_____
_____
_____
_____

How did it feel when I moved away from home?

_____
_____
_____
_____
_____
_____
_____
_____
_____
_____
_____

What should I know about having children?

_____
_____
_____
_____
_____
_____
_____
_____
_____
_____
_____
_____
_____
_____
_____
_____
_____
_____
_____
_____
_____
_____
_____

All about you...

What do you love to do?

_____

_____

_____

_____

_____

_____

_____

_____

_____

_____

_____

_____

_____

_____

_____

_____

_____

_____

_____

_____

_____

_____

What is your favorite flower?

"EARTH LAUGHS IN FLOWERS."
Ralph Waldo Emerson

What is your favorite quote?

Write down a favorite family recipe. Where did you get it?

EAT & BE HAPPY

MILK

FLOUR

PURE VANILLA EXTRACT

If you could be any age again, which would you choose?

_____

_____

_____

_____

_____

_____

_____

_____

_____

_____

_____

_____

_____

_____

_____

_____

_____

_____

_____

_____

"Backward, turn backward, O Time in your flight;
Make me a child again just for tonight." ♥

Elizabeth Akers Allen

Where have you traveled that you loved the best? Tell me why.

What's the best place you have ever lived?

BLESSINGS
LOVE

A house is made of walls & beams; a home is built with love & dreams.

What's your secret food addiction?

"THINGS TASTE
BETTER
IN
SMALL HOUSES."
Queen Victoria

What's a favorite piece of jewelry you own? Where did you get it?

What was the most surprising gift you ever received?

The best gifts are tied with heartstrings.

Who are your heroes?

If you could do it all over, would you change anything?

What would you most like to be remembered for?

_____

_____

_____

_____

_____

_____

_____

_____

_____

_____

_____

_____

_____

_____

_____

_____

_____

_____

_____

"God has given us our memories
that we might have roses in December."

♥ J. M. Barrie

What advice about life would you love to give but know I don't want to hear?

What makes you happiest?

LIFE IS GOOD

What is the most important thing you have learned?

THE BEST THINGS IN LIFE AREN'T THINGS.

More stories...

A picture goes here;
your family, your house,
your dog, your cat —
but best would be
YOU
since this is your book. ♥

"All that mankind has done, thought or been:
it is in magic preservation, in the pages of books."
❤ THOMAS CARLYLE

_____

Sign your name

_____

Date

❤